A Ballad of Life,

Anchorages,

and

Other Poems

Martin Brown

Wuggles Publishing,
Clydach, Swansea, South Wales.

ISBN 978- 1- 904043- 18 8

A Ballad of Life,

Anchorages,

and

Other Poems

Martin Brown

CONTENTS

Part I: A Ballad of Life and Other Poems

Part II: Anchorages: Poems on the Cusp of Other Things

All men dream: but not equally.
Those who dream by night in the
dusty recesses of their minds wake
in the day to find that it was vanity:
but the dreamers of the day are
dangerous men, for they may act
their dream with open eyes, to make
it possible.

Seven Pillars of Wisdom
T. E. Lawrence

Part I:

A Ballad of Life

and

Other Poems

A Ballad of Life

Of all the things
We have to pay for,
Wasting one's time
Must be the worst.

And of all that is most irrelevant
When you are dead and gone
Must be
The lightness of your purse.

So pay the scroungers, pay the fools,
Pay your taxes if you must,
But don't let them consume your legacy
That will continue when you're dust.

For when you're dead
What will you leave
By participating in this
Mindless scrum of greed?

The vultures will gather
And divide up what's left,
After all of the scrounging
And legally criminal government theft.

But you'll have your gravestone
Where your ISBN is wearing away,
Forgotten by the scroungers
Who politely stole all your money today.

What Price a Feline Dream?

What price a feline dream?
A whisker-twitching adventure
That happens without moving
When the world is still and serene.

What price a warm embrace
When the night is cold?
The heat of two bodies felt as one,
And of love reflected in a face?

What price an errant line
So perfect in itself alone?
That naturally leads to others
And completed with the truth of rhyme?

What price an hour alone
To do nothing but clear the mind to think?
To usher in the dawn of beauty,
Something valuable done.

What price a feline dream?
A paw-trembling adventure
That happens without moving
When the world is still and serene.

Inspiration

Not sought for
But coming of their own accord
The lines pour forth
From pen to page unforced.

Poetry flows from my pen like ink
As if ink were poetry
And poetry ink.

The meanings gather
And strive to fill every pore
And miniscule imperfection in the page,
Like the sea feels and searches out
Every cave and fissure –
Even those invisible to the eye alone.

And when all has been explored
(Or so I think)
I retreat and wait
For another line to,
Unsuspecting,
Wander by . . .

Dylan's Song

Dylan's soft Welsh rhythms and lilting
words
Caress you and wander
Like warm winds or sinuous rills,
And you follow where they take you,
Back to your childhood, back to Fern
Hill.

And the sun shines majestic,
And the moon is floating
Like a shining sixpence in the sky,
You can almost feel that the grass is
waving
As if to say goodbye,
But life is bred by Dylan's song
And you feel you'll never die.

You will roam your hills forever
And talk with whispering streams,
Where the rain will help your spirit grow
The wind will dry your hair,
And neither will interrupt your dreams.

The Echo Resounding

An artist without an audience
Is only a maker of things
Bereft of a point.
Like having a conversation with oneself,
You practice for an opportunity
When someone may listen.

I stood at the gates to the world
And announced my intentions.
Awaiting a response
I simply heard the echo resounding,
Bouncing and rebounding off
The world's stony indifference.

An echo is a lonely sound:
The echo from a writer's pen
Is a disembodied sound
Looking for a refuge,
Where it may become art
And fulfil its purpose.

The echo resounds
Off every closed door and mind,
And seems captured within
Every envelope,
Whose contents thank me politely
For my wasted efforts.

If my echo still resounds
Then I suppose I must
Continue renewing my echo
In ever deepening and resonant caverns,
Practicing for an opportunity
When someone may listen.

The Wish to be Buried at an Angle

As I look at the gravestones
In their neat, tidy rows
(In death as in life)
I think I would like to be buried at an angle
(For even the enclosed sheep are dotted
In irregular patterns about the fields)
So I may look directly over the hills to the blue Irish Sea.

A rolling green landscape of hedgerows and trees
Would be the view that I'd have forever,
Only Nature herself can create so many greens
And combine them with such imperfections of beauty.

Interrupted by clumpy woodlands
And set afire by yellow gorse,

The zephyred silence is trilled away by
the warbling birds.
The great flat sea, blue as the sky,
Stretches sublime to the horizon,
Only streamed apart by a lighter steering
its course –
Like a tiny blip on the radar of universal
time.

The huge wind turbines
They are building in the Bay of
Liverpool
Are made to wave by Nature's breath
alone,
As if to remind all humankind
That we must all wave goodbye
To the energy of life – eventually.

If I were to die tomorrow
And knew that I would be buried here
With a view of my own, that can't be
taxed
Or swindled away from me,

I would happily embrace the turning of
the day
And march with hope towards eternity.

Message In A Bottle

At the bottom of every bottle
There lies an answer
Whose worth must be questionable,
If you consider
That it has been plumbed
From so shallow a depth.

The message in the bottle
Bobs on the sea –
Now there, now hidden –
Separated from the depths
In its false container . . .

let it out
let it fall
let it down
let it glide around
and down –
suspended –
without end –
until the bottom is found.

The answer gained . . . .
What then?

At the bottom of every bottle
There lies a question,
Which asks: “Do you really want
“To know what the answer is?”

Poem for a Girl

My own girl with the sky-blue hair
Calls so quiet and sweet to me
That I hardly hear her say
Her sweet and gentle things,
That proved to me
That her heart was gentle too.

No need for self-promotion
Or bluster of great things
Her voice just speaks a confidence
Borne up on angel's wings.

But though she may be far away
Our love will make the distance short,
I will see the lustre in her eyes
And her voice on sunlit winds was
caught,
And carried to me by Nature's force.

Epipsychidion 2008

I looked into your eyes
And asked you to accompany
This strange and disjointed man
To his sylvan bower of poetry.

Each vessel needs an anchor,
For though it loves to wander free,
It needs a quiet bay to rest within
Between adventures on the seas.

And though the ship may never be
grounded,
Though it may founder in the lee,
The anchor will still be aboard,
Like fuel, a reminder of mortality.

You know never to drop the anchor
When the winds are in the sheets
Not to interrupt the onward flow
Lest the pen may miss a heartbeat.

Blood is ink and ink is in my blood,
That you understand,
And you know that it may dry up
Or cascade in torrent and flood –
And, when thus, I break free of land
You know I'm bound for sea,
And I know that if you influence these thoughts
It's just a loving act of piracy.

Rouxe

Rouxe, my love,
At least lie your love
For me, my love;
So that, when I am dead,
And my heart lies within me broken,
It won't be for the want of three small words
Your lips had never spoken.

When the roaring elements
Have worn away
The hills and mountains of my native Wales,
And all that remains behind
Is a desert waste of barren shale,
The only signs of life left upon it
Will be the scattered fragments of my broken heart,
Still beating with my love for you
A thousand years from now.

Nourished by the hope
That comes from your pretty, pretty lies,
And beauty's poison love
That still regards me with a stranger's
eyes.

Love

I make love to you
And you to me
We be.
We are
Afloat around amongst the stars.
So close, yet so tragically far,
I melt inside
Around and within you,
Gliding in the dark night ocean of your soul.

Down and around I float and hear no sound –
Except your breathing –
Like the distant rush of waves on the shore . . .
Shhh . . . shhh . . . shhh –
"Go to sleep,
And give your dreams wholly to me,
Swim the ocean of your soul –
Give yourself up to the sea."

Like a lunar gymnast
I give myself up to the rhythms of you
Floating in pure joy –
That which we experience
But cannot grasp –
It slips through my fingers like water.

A place of wish . . .
I would be a fish . . .
And float inside you . . .
Forever –
And see the blue
The beautiful, all-encompassing blue
Sprinkled with glittering diamond
sunlight.

I would glide and move so perfectly
within you
I would become water –
An idea within your soul
With all the bright neon-coloured fish
Which flit and dart
Like lightning ballet.

I am floating around and down –
I wheel around –
There is no sound –
Except the gentle rush . . .
I drown.
In you I flow
I die, I die
But what a way to go.

Rejection

Pick yourself up off the floor,
You are not needed anymore.
Put you away
But keep you in store
Back in your box and lock the door,
You are not wanted anymore.

So we can let you shout,
To be told you are happy and wanted
Until we have had our fun and can
Tell you to get back out.
You are not wanted anymore.

Take your things and make your way
To somewhere else,
That is where you belong.
You are not wanted here anymore –
We fail to see what use you are for.

Take your good manners,
Take your kindness and good intentions,
They are not wanted anymore.

Look into my kind, lying eyes
And see the message written there.
You are not wanted anymore.

One More Disaster Away

Just one more disaster away.
Just one more disaster away
From the end.
And then mercy – it will stop.

But do I, in a perverse human way,
Like this happening –
Is it there to remind me
That I am?
And would I miss it if I didn't –
Or wasn't?

Still the rain falls . . .
It seeps into my failing mind
Through rotted seals
And shattered gaskets.
It erodes my inner strength
With its constant drip, drip, drip, –
As persistent as the ticking of a clock –
My resistance wears away
Until I face what lies beneath
The fragile veneer of sanity –

The terror of the reality
Of the choice
That lies
At the bottom
Of every life.

Like the bravery of the military hero
Who has nothing left to live for,
Mine is a frightening and reckless thing.
A terrifying and chaotic freedom
That threatens to produce the ultimate anarchy –
Just one more disaster away.

This precarious fragility of being
Ought to make life more precious –
But when the mind becomes unhinged –
Disconnected –
From worn-out reasoning –
Afloat, barely,
Upon a storm
In which the vessel cannot cope –
A freak wave –
A sudden surge and swell –

Just one more disaster away.

And then . . . cast away from
Your sadly inadequate craft
You struggle against the waves alone
Until, your last resistance gone,
You know it is useless to fear what has
become inevitable –
The hero's bravery
Allows the sea-salt evil in
To invade and consume,
Envelope and choke –
Just one more disaster away –
You experience the final terror
Of truly not caring.

The Dawn

When the first light appears
The birds awake and start to sing
A freshness lies upon the world
Untroubled as yet by human things.

The dawn is the best time to be alive
When the world is quiet and calm,
Life is new and full of hope
The mind soothed with nature's balm.

But birdsong is soon beaten down
By the twisted song of human life,
The feeling of the dawn grows tired
And is replaced by toil and strife.

But when the sticky sweat of day is over
And evening gathers up what's left
And scatters it to goodness
As if goodness were now bereft,
The birds fly out and pick it up
Like material for a nest
To make of it all what they may
And create the dawn of another day.

The Right Honourable Gentleman

The Right Honourable Gentleman
Is addressed in the House
Which is not a house at all.
Neither is the man a gentleman.

The fact that he is Right all the time
Should not blind us to the fact
Of his storehouse of statistics
That fuels his specious response.

But if the evidence of the country
Should prove him actually to be wrong,
He will still be Right in the House
Which is not a house at all.

And if his financial affairs
Should prove dishonourable,
And his political dealings
Should turn out the same,
He will still be addressed as Honourable
And continue the in-house game.

So when he is addressed in the House
Which is not a house at all,
Everyone should search around
And wonder where this person is?

But if we should think he is a nobody
He will certainly prove us wrong,
For he has "The" left
(The definite article)
Just to prove he hasn't gone.

A Universal Panacea for a Different World

I see the children come from shacks
The teachers from their bland concrete box,
They wear their coats in the classroom
Because the heating is off again.
There is no political argument
No disagreement with what is said –
This is not "democracy."

They may not have a TV set –
But each of them shows due respect
And each is keen to learn in school,
About what is valuable.

We may think they live in squalor,
But they decorate their houses with poetry
And fill their boards with food –
The happy smiling family
Makes the concrete feel almost good.

Poor and backward nation!
Please donate your TV set,
And give them your money
So they can eat at McDonalds
And enjoy the privilege of the West –
Because surely that is best.

They must surely be unhappy
Without our gadgets and our fads.
It's as if someone has taken away
All that is best for human life.

The only things the poor people
Are left with are their
Pride, honour, and respect –
Things that we regard,
If we regard them at all,
As things of the past in the West.

Bench

(an affirmation upon the life and death of Sophie Lancaster, prompted by the dedication of a bench to her memory on the West Cliff, Whitby, April 2008)

What is the meaning of a simple bench
Beyond that of the elements
From which it's comprised? –
The bench is simply slats of wood
Bound by iron straps –
A personal and universal meaning
Determined by the self and not others.
And for those that think
The meaning is indeed elementary,
As if it may prove that
From all our lives
Something lasting may be produced.

A peaceful spot surrounded by the world
You would never fully know –
A suitable spot of freedom for the soul
to run free.

Let the wind breathe life
Through the sinews of the soul,
And the sun warm the heart.
Let the real attachment of the ground
Hold you steady,
To contemplate the freedom ahead and
above.

Sweet flowers on the bench
What is it that you say to me
That makes me cry so hard?
From a girl I never knew I take hope . . .

The Whitby harbour moles reach out their arms to sea, as if to embrace the world and what lies ahead . . .

The Only World There Is

I wondered, when I was working away:
Is this the only world there is?

I think of the people I know
And what they are doing now:
Shows to packed houses
In Arizona and Germany.

So why am I here? Tramping about
Wrapped up against the cold and rain
With a hole in my coat
And a scruffy old bag?

I think of all the people filed away
In their little labelled boxes,
In hiding
From something they don't understand –
Something scary and different –
Behind their bay windows
Busied
Paying all their bills.

And I wonder if they also think:
Is this the only world there is?

When people talk of security
I think of money,
Locked up in vans,
That isn't mine –
Inaccessible –
I think of things secured
With padlocks and chains –
Animals and Nature restrained by bars –
Or behind bay windows,
That are guarded by people
Who make rules for themselves;
And whose favourite words
Are "don't" and "can't."

Is it important or worthwhile
To perpetuate this silly system,
Whose only justification
Comes from the mouths of those it has
duped?

But they would argue
That it is necessary that there be
This silent money-circulating majority –
But the tree falls in the woods
And nobody hears it
Because nobody is there –
Then it ceases to be important at all.

A world of posters and sounds
And people who shout and scream
And dance around –
Is that not a reality too?
But that reality is not for you:
Because what surrounds you
Are the endless toasters
And grounds of beige
That hem you in
And impose their reality
Upon you from above –
Where you are below.

But smash away this weak façade
Of facile argument and mundanity
And reveal the real possibilities
That are open to you:
Discover!
This is not the only world there is.

The Dreamcat-cher

Furry black pudding
Professional dreamer
Study in repose.
Nothing to give away
Signs of life
Except whiskers twitching
About the nose.

Spasm-footed dreamer
Chasing dreams –
When you are sitting motionless
Thinking –
Plans you will hatch
And dreams you will catch.

Furry black pudding
Professional dreamer
Chaser in repose.
You have nothing to give away –
Unless of course you catch your dreams,
Then you can give away those.

You could sleep beside my bedside
And when I begin to dream
You could snare them in your puss-cat
catching net.
And when I awoke in the morning
I could rummage in your net
And pick the dreams I liked the most
And take them with me to work each
day
To brighten the humdrum
And help me believe
That something better may be possible.

Dreams may not come true
But they are such pretty, pretty lies
That you want them to lie to you again
and again –
Like a girl who says she loves you.

Furry black pudding
Catcher of dreams
Seer of life's dark flow.
Furry black pudding
Inscrutable schemer
Feline know.

Freedom of Thought: A Ballad of the Universe

If God looked on his universe
Imagine what he'd see,
A million billion tiny points of light
Each a galaxy.

And within each tiny point of light
A million more he'd see,
And of six billion dots on one of those
One might be you or me.

Part II:

Anchorages:

Poems on the Cusp of Other Things

Anchorages

These anchors tie me fast
And prevent me from moving on;
They all seemed good ideas at the time,
Each one

drags me down,
And prevents me from roaming free.
Drowning creativity.
Preventing me from being me.

These chains are sometimes hard to
sever,
But sever them I must
And soon, before I grow old,
And lose my lust

for life will pass away from me –
And before I've given myself a chance
Death will come for the reckoning
With his newly-whetted scythe,
To finally cut these anchor chains
And sever me from life.

Khali I

I wish that you would say
To me what you felt today
When you looked into my eyes
So vibrant and alive
You seemed, as if you loved me.

Your eyes flash at me their elfin-fire
beauty
The yellow-green pools in which I
would bathe,
I hang on your whispered sibilance
Like a heart hung out to try again
What little luck it can find
In the torture game of life and love.

And if everything were where it ought to
be
You would be in my arms
And love me forever
As I would love you – and you alone –
Whatever.

Khali II

I looked into your yellow-green eyes
And saw my happiness reflected there.
But Khali's eyes, they lied to me –
Perhaps that is what I wanted to see –
And my love was only projected there.

It seems that I invented you
And thought the patent pending
For your elfin, pure simplicity
So perfectly suited to me.
The start of a story never-ending.

A woman distilled into her purest form
I seemed to ignore your innate human complexity
Or the fact you might choose someone else,
Which you did.

I search continually for an illusion, it
seems –
For the girl I see in dreams –
Whom I try to make reality
In a seemingly vain attempt
To make myself happy.

Happiness is a means and not an end
And I simply look to progress
But without the tools I cannot do the job
–
My life must remain unfulfilled –
Incomplete.

Replete with disappointment I trudge on
Simply keeping pace with time,
Until I reach the end of the line?

The River

Down by where the lilies grow
I met my lover today –
I looked deep into her eyes –
Which were somehow different from
What they looked like yesterday.

She had met me here
To say she didn't want me anymore.
And all the things I had to say,
As I stared deep into the river,
Were left in silence, to be poured
uselessly away.

And the water washes away
Their meanings, become mumbles
Meaningless and ridiculous,
From their context untimely ripped,
I feel like a ridiculous man
Laughable in his presumption,
Who becomes miserly with his feelings:
Closed and tight-lipped.

Unrequited Love

When the one you love
Loves you not in return
They do not feel the aching, sickening emptiness
Or the tears on your face that run and burn.

No matter that you are good,
The qualities she values are a mystery to you –
And probably a mystery to her –
But you know she does not love you.

You are the victim
But no-one is to blame
The perpetrator is simply life
Playing its little game.

The line of tears sears the wrinkles in your face
So that, when you are an old man, and you meet her again –

As young and pretty and vibrant as she
is today –
You can show her the lines
That are a tribute to,
And a tributary of,
The love she couldn't find for you.

A Girl

Find me a girl
Who knows what I mean
When I'm saying my usual things: -
And who won't think them
Too hair-brained or erudite.

And if she has a body
That suggests that the gods were
Pouring milk
On the day they created her –
That would be good too.

And please let her know
When I'm joking or serious
So that the laughs come
In the right places.

And if you are wondering
Whether I'm asking too much?
However unlikely it may seem to some –
There is still a good chance
That of all of the people

Crammed into the world –
She may well be here somewhere.

And if I can do nothing
More active to make her happy,
Than to stroke her hair
And hold her when she is asleep –
Then at least I can believe
That her dreams have been made
happier.

You

You are the sun that rises in the morning
You are the blood pulsing through my
veins
You are the river running to the sea
The mountains raised by tectonic plates
You are the monsoon rains.

You are the stream running through my
fingers
The wind that blows through my hair
You are the wind in the trees
The trees in the fields
The life-giving breath of air.

The spirit that binds my being to life
And binds it to life itself
You are the sunset that ends the day
The clock that ticks within me
The beautiful darkness that lights my
way.

The Lovers' Tree

I love you and you love me
Here we sit beneath the lovers' tree,
And if love so blinds us that we may not see
Beyond each other, then let it be,
Because I love you and you love me
And we sit beneath the lovers' tree.

Once this tree was but a planted seed,
Like the flash of love in your eye,
Our thoughts journeyed wild and free
To fathom out love's mystery.
But love so blinded us that we could not see
Beyond our dual immediacy,
For I loved you and you loved me
And we sat together beneath the lovers' tree.

Chalford Hill

Six inches fell last night
And softened the world in a cloak of
white.
Nature dictated the people postpone their
greed
And people, for once, took heed of
Nature.
So children stayed at home
To learn different lessons.

All is becalmed in the soft snow sea,
Bounded in by Nature's will,
The peaks and troughs of stress and
depression
Are filled in and evened out,
Five hundred feet up on Chalford Hill.

It is as if Nature had sent cold
To increase the human desire for warmth
The snow insulates us against the
outside world
And a sense of community grows.

Normally people don't say hello
But now they do, and smile,
When they're bounded in by snow: –
Their childlike sense of play
And fair-play separates them from adult life
Like the village is today.

The snow falls still on Chalford Hill –
And it floats through the winter sky
Like the ash from a cold volcano,
Trying to clog the narrow lanes
Trapping experience and memory still,
Between the buildings of frozen mustard Cotswold stone –
And between those who live on Chalford Hill.

The spectrum of colour
Descends the cloudless sky to the black horizon.
The ghost-grey silhouettes of the apple trees,
Dressed in their best snow clothes,

Watch the last faint rays of the setting
sun
Make the snow crystals in the orchard
twinkle
Like the stars in the galaxies above.

Reciprocity

One tear on a mirror, two tears I see,
One tear for you, and one for me;
And as it runs it blurs my face
Distorting my identity.

We have to agree to disagree
One tear on a mirror, two tears I see,
A cathartic reciprocity –
The best we can manage in the twenty-
first century

An Argument on the Despair of Life

It doesn't matter
In the great scheme of things,
If a scheme there be,
Because who will care about
The love I could never find
A hundred years from now? –
Unless they read the poetry
That claims it doesn't matter –
Unless they believe the poem
That claims it doesn't matter.

But everything must matter
In the here and now –
Even to the writer of these lines –
Otherwise nothing will matter
And there will be no history
To care about me at all.

Therefore, it is not the meaning or
purpose of
experience that I deny,
But the futile attempt to deny the hurt it
produces –
Which must be a denial of existence
itself.

It does matter that she does not love me,
It must matter that she does not love me
–
I must have the pain and frustration
that makes me a human being –
I must engage with the feelings which
I think will destroy me
But will in reality do me no harm –
I will do that.

If I embrace the pain of experience
As being necessary to human life,
Then self-destruction must be
impossible.

Train Journey:
Colwyn Bay to Dublin

Over the river
To the walls of Conwy Castle
Where old friends depart
And others board like new ideas or
episodes.

The stippled sea around Penmaenmawr
Is crumpled like a bed sheet,
Where night once slept.
The baggy-faced girl sitting opposite
Smiles at the banter of the kids from St
Gerrard's –
So young they have no conception
Of the old thoughts in my head –
I wonder how old they think I am?

They disembark at Bangor, and more
come aboard –
Another change and turn –
Across the straits to Llanfairpwll
And the great flatlands of Anglesey.

Hedgerows and fields
And trees and hedgerows
And fields and hedgerows and trees
Flash by the window, as time flees.

The train slashes Anglesey
Into uneven halves
On its journey to Holyhead,
For embarkation on the sea.

When all you have to look at
Is the next hill over
Life and the world can seem small,
But when you venture out to sea
Upon whose fathomless depths you
hover –
The depths and heights
The distance and depths
The heights and distance and depths,
That crawl by like a moment's thought –
You gain a more sublime impression
Of our placement
Here on Earth.

A sense of great perspective
That shows how small we are –
How silly are our everyday problems –
I mount the waves
Like I enter a cathedral –
The majesty above,
The hidden depths of meaning,
The thoughts that ride the waves –
Off into the distance – far, far away.

Twitterings

The twitterings of birds which suddenly erupt
From Nature, as if disembodied
Utterings of an ultimate freedom –
Even freed from mortal bounds –
Makes my heart beat fast with joy,
As if there is something to strive for –
An example only experienced here,
As other things bind you in to towns
Where even the birds chirrup a forlorn hope
From lonely trees
And fool themselves, like us, that all this is good.

Nature

I still feel close to Nature –
The pale yellow winter sunset
Reflected in the Menai Straits –
Where the random shapes of clouds
Would please no office manager.

I project my feelings outwards
Beyond the confines of four blank walls
–
The restrictions and rules we place on
ourselves
Within a free and open universe
To some seem to quell some danger.

If I was asked which I would choose,
The sound of diesel engines or birdsong?
I would only answer for the birds
If they had lived away from humankind
On an island amidst a million acres of
sea
Unexplored, or deep within a mountain
wilderness,

Or even in a sylvan glade,
Just far enough away to be sheltered
from
The buzz, and noise, and hullabaloo,
Which sidetracks, stresses, and distracts
From what ought to be done
And that which we would laugh at
If we saw it done by others.

Launderette

Launderette.
A contradictory word
That seems to sum up
And encapsulate
All that is small in life.

The whirling, colourful drum,
The somnambulent hum,
The vacant look,
The endless money
Pumped into the machine,
To make it all nice and bearable,
And squeaky clean.

List

Abraham Lincoln.
Mohandas K. Gandhi.
John Fitzgerald Kennedy.
Martin Luther King Jr.
John Winston Lennon.

"I have a dream:" – "give peace a chance."

Jesus Christ.

Epiphany on a Hill

Climb to the top of a hill in Wales
And heaven awaits you there.
You look down across the gorse-filled
heath
And green-squared fields;
You see the great blue sea –
Which makes you feel so small –
Dwarfed only by the sky's blue canopy
So seemingly close, like a warm blanket
It protects us against the lonely universe.

So high up you may see Liverpool Bay
Beyond the farthest shore of Puffin
Island –
It makes me feel small and impotent,
A tiny creature in amongst this world –
I suddenly feel powerless to achieve –
Though that indeed is what we all are –
Those who scurry and rush below –
And their swindlings suddenly count for
nothing.

To Epictetus

who pointed out that human beings have two ears, but only one mouth, for the purposes of communication

Those who listen are always
Less noticeable
Than those who shout and interrupt
And try to drag you down,
Instead of being buoyed up
On a cushion of silence.

Shankland Reading Room

Shankland Reading Room
Echoes a time of safe simplicity –
Of work with impunity
Before life's disillusionment begins –
The longer you stay, the worse it
becomes.

Here you are offered no guarantees –
No tax incentives, pension schemes,
No pointless secret give and take –
The armorial bearings printed high on
the ceiling
Look down; grand, hopeless, and
forlorn.

A vacuum of stillness and quiet amidst
The chaotic, turbulent world –
A place where culture, heritage, and
tradition are valued –
A beautiful place to work.

The dusty flies vibrate quietly against
the windows
And the books lie, humming with
knowledge,
Like the excited riffling heartbeat of
pages –
So much potential –
So much of the past, and of the future.

So far up, up and away –
You only faintly hear the engines of the
Sporadic cars on College Road . . .

Thirty-five Summers

I trudge along a country lane alone
Away from what the world may do –
Will it be forever so?
Beset by the imperfections of human
life;

Thirty-five summers have passed and,
God willing, thirty-five more my lot;
And when I finally close my eyes
Will the sky still be as blue?
And will my heart still hold some hope?
For all these little creatures
Making their little pointless to do?

The Dream of the Poet

The strangest thing occurred last night
An angel in a flash of light
Appeared to me in a dream
And said to me, or so it seemed,
That I would make a sacrifice –
That I would give up my life
And would set about to bestow –
Even on those who increase my woes –
A nugget of golden wisdom mined,
For those willing to listen,
Like scattered diamonds in logic's
sunlight glisten.

The Money-Spider

I saw a money-spider today –
He was walking across my desk –
Then he climbed upon my pen –
Then he went away again.

I didn't do him any harm
I helped him on his way –
It hasn't brought me any luck
. . . yet . . .
But a money-spider climbed upon my
pen today.

Llinos

She is as light and fun and colourful
As the balloons she chases and bursts.
Such fun as she has is infectious –
Above all other things, her fun comes first.

Her attitude is jubilant,
Her spirit is buoyant and free,
And of all the people at the party
She sits and talks to me.

The Death of the Artist

We all search for our spot in life
But I for mine in death,
For I will even spit words in blood
With my dying breath.

I will reproduce the pages
Which will live beyond my years –
So, my friends, look after my children
And make sure that everyone hears.

I cast my progeny upon
The often vicious waves of life
And perhaps I should take greater care –
But if they're to survive at all
Amongst human pettiness and strife
They'll learn the lessons there.

I do not work for money
But for a life in death –
An artist to rest in a work of art
Of sufficient scope and breadth
To do honour to my genius
When I am dead.

Let not my soul be turbulent,
Let me be happy that
I have drunk fully from the cups of life –
Sweet and bitter alike.

Death moves me: –
I cry when I feel some truth
Because it reminds me of
The greatest truth I know –
I will die –
And in what state we approach it
Is the work of these, our lives.

Let all that could be done
Have been done.
Let all that could be loved
Have been loved.
Let all that could have been
Have come about.
And let all that could have been said
Have been said – and said well.

Let not my soul be regretful
Of thoughts that weren't expressed,
Of closest friends misunderstood,
Of problems unaddressed –
And look kindly upon my intentions
For they were sincerely for the best.

Lightning Source UK Ltd.
Milton Keynes UK
30 December 2010

165042UK00001B/4/P

9 781904 043188